THE WHALE SHARK

By Megan Borgert-Spaniol

BELLWETHER MEDIA • MINNEAPOLIS, MN

Jump into the cockpit and take flight with Pilot books. Your journey will take you on high-energy adventures as you learn about all that is wild, weird, fascinating, and fun!

This edition first published in 2013 by Bellwether Media, Inc.

No part of this publication may be reproduced in whole or in part without written permission of the publisher. For information regarding permission, write to Bellwether Media, Inc., Attention: Permissions Department, 5357 Penn Avenue South, Minneapolis, MN 55419.

Library of Congress Cataloging-in-Publication Data

Borgert-Spaniol, Megan, 1989-
 The whale shark / by Megan Borgert-Spaniol.
    p. cm. – (Pilot books: shark fact files)
 Includes bibliographical references and index.
 Summary: "Engaging images accompany information about the whale shark. The combination of high-interest subject matter and narrative text is intended for students in grades 3 through 7"–Provided by publisher.
 ISBN 978-1-60014-807-1 (hardcover : alk. paper)
 1. Whale shark–Juvenile literature. I. Title.
 QL638.95.R4B67 2013
 597.3'3–dc23
                    2012001698

TABLE OF CONTENTS

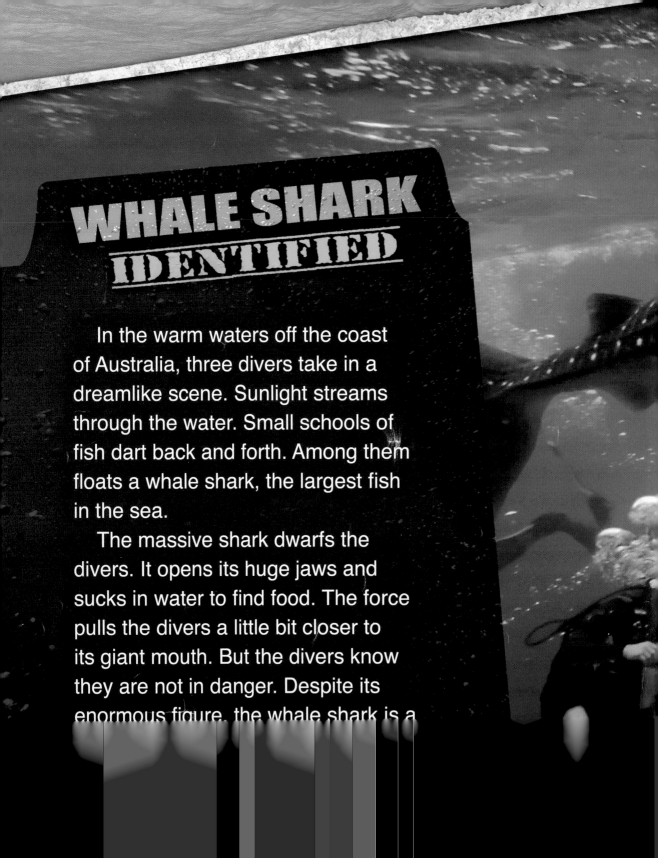

WHALE SHARK
IDENTIFIED

In the warm waters off the coast of Australia, three divers take in a dreamlike scene. Sunlight streams through the water. Small schools of fish dart back and forth. Among them floats a whale shark, the largest fish in the sea.

The massive shark dwarfs the divers. It opens its huge jaws and sucks in water to find food. The force pulls the divers a little bit closer to its giant mouth. But the divers know they are not in danger. Despite its enormous figure, the whale shark is a

MAKE NO MISTAKE

Whales are mammals, and sharks are fish. The whale shark is a fish named simply for its large size.

Whale sharks live across the globe in every tropical ocean and sea except the Mediterranean. They are usually found at or near the surface of the open sea. Patterns of pale spots and stripes cover their gray or brown backs. Their bellies are all white. This countershading helps them blend in with sunlit ocean waters.

whale shark   human

The whale shark can measure more than 40 feet (12 meters) long and weigh more than 30,000 pounds (13,600 kilograms). Its skeleton is made of cartilage. This helps the shark move gracefully through the water. The caudal fin helps propel the shark forward as the rear part of its body moves slowly from side to side. Two dorsal fins and two pectoral fins help the shark balance and steer.

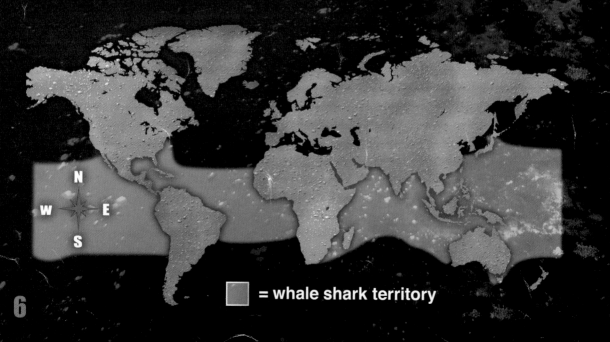

N
W   E
S

☐ = whale shark territory

WHALE SHARK I.D.

Every whale shark sports a unique pattern of spots and stripes. Scientists use the patterns to identify individual whale sharks.

WHALE SHARK
TRACKED

Until 1995, most researchers believed that whale sharks grew in eggs outside their mothers' bodies. This belief changed with the discovery of a female whale shark in Taiwan. Hundreds of pups were found growing inside her. Now whale sharks are thought to be ovoviviparous. This means they develop in egg cases inside their mothers.

Whale sharks mainly live alone after they are born. However, smaller fish often hover on their backs or under their bellies. They use the whale sharks as protective shields.

plankton

COME ONE, COME ALL

The largest known gathering of whale sharks takes place off the Yucatán Peninsula in Mexico. Schools of over 400 whale sharks have been spotted in these plankton-rich waters.

Whale sharks migrate in search of food. This sometimes brings hundreds of whale sharks to the same food source. They seek out plankton.

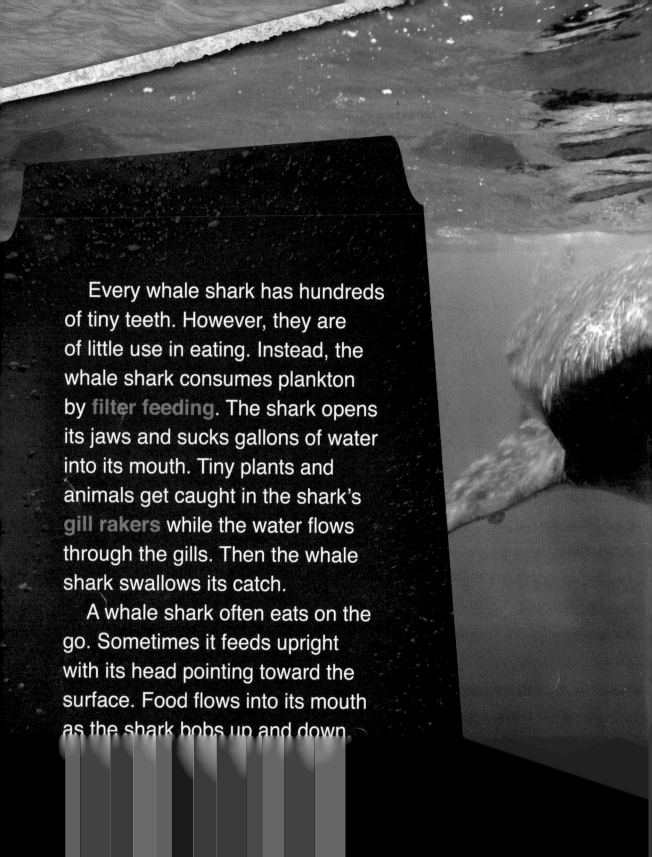

Every whale shark has hundreds of tiny teeth. However, they are of little use in eating. Instead, the whale shark consumes plankton by **filter feeding**. The shark opens its jaws and sucks gallons of water into its mouth. Tiny plants and animals get caught in the shark's **gill rakers** while the water flows through the gills. Then the whale shark swallows its catch.

A whale shark often eats on the go. Sometimes it feeds upright with its head pointing toward the surface. Food flows into its mouth as the shark bobs up and down.

AHEM!

Too much plankton can clog a whale shark's gill rakers. When this happens, a whale shark coughs to clear its throat!

Whale sharks also like to snack on fish eggs. When snapper fish release their eggs into the water, whale sharks are nearby to fill up on the tiny prey. In fact, they are known to travel long distances for fish eggs. The coral spawning off the coast of Australia attracts many whale sharks every April. When plankton or fish eggs are not enough, a hungry whale shark may scoop up sardines, squid, or tuna. Anything larger is too big to swallow whole.

The whale shark uses sensors to lead it to food. The ampullae of Lorenzini cluster around the shark's snout. They can detect the electric fields of nearby prey. Nasal openings allow the whale shark to hunt by smell. Barbels extend from above the nostrils. They sense movement in water and guide the shark's mouth toward prey.

14

Young whale sharks are easy targets for quick predators like blue sharks, orcas, and marlins. Predators are less likely to attack adult whale sharks because of their size. If they do, a whale shark's skin offers protection. It can be over 4 inches (10 centimeters) thick. If damaged, it can heal completely over time. This protection allows the whale shark to live up to 100 years.

WHALE SHARK
CURRENT STATUS

The whale shark's biggest threat is humans. In the past it was common for fishers to harpoon whale sharks. The meat would be eaten fresh or salted. Oil from the shark's liver was used to waterproof boats. Today whale shark fishing is not allowed in India, the Philippines, and a few other countries. However, the practice is still legal in many Asian countries. Fishers are especially interested in whale shark fins. They sell at a high price for use in shark fin soup.

The whale shark is legally protected in Australia, the Maldives, Mexico, and other countries that want to see the shark thrive. These countries support ecotourism programs that feature whale sharks and their habitat. Tourists can spot the massive form of a whale shark as it glides past their boat. Snorkelers can swim just feet away from the gentle giants.

Most ecotourism programs take care not to disturb whale sharks. Divers may be tempted to touch the friendly fish or even hitch a ride. However, this can break the protective coating on the shark's skin and cause infection. Boaters must watch out for whale sharks that swim just below the surface. Some whale sharks have scars or damaged fins from boat propellers.

propeller injury

SHARK BRIEF

Common Name: Whale Shark

Nickname: Domino

Claim to Fame: Largest fish in the sea

Hot Spots:
Southern Japan
Eastern Thailand
The Philippines
Western Australia
Gulf of Mexico
Galapagos Islands
Southeastern Africa
Southern India

Life Span: 60 to 100 years

Current Status: Vulnerable (IUCN)

EXTINCT

EXTINCT IN THE WILD

CRITICALLY ENDANGERED

ENDANGERED

VULNERABLE

NEAR THREATENED

LEAST CONCERN

Researchers believe the number of whale sharks in the ocean is decreasing. Whale sharks do not reproduce often, and overfishing is a constant threat. This means the population will likely continue its decline. The International Union for Conservation of Nature (IUCN) has given the whale shark a vulnerable rating.

Meanwhile, people learn more about whale sharks
every day. At the Okinawa Churaumi Aquarium in Japan,
a glass panel spanning almost 75 feet (23 meters) is all
that separates visitors from an underwater world. Three
whale sharks swim among the manta rays and schools of
fish. Tourists gaze up in awe as they discover the peace
and beauty of the whale shark, a true ocean wonder.

GLOSSARY

ampullae of Lorenzini—a network of tiny jelly-filled sacs around a shark's snout; the jelly is sensitive to the electric fields of nearby prey.

barbels—finger-like extensions above the whale shark's nostrils

cartilage—firm, flexible connective tissue that makes up a shark's skeleton

caudal fin—the tail fin of a fish

countershading—coloring that helps camouflage an animal; fish with countershading have pale bellies and dark backs.

dorsal fins—the fins on the back of a fish

ecotourism—the practice of allowing tourists to safely observe wildlife without disturbing it

electric fields—waves of electricity created by movement; every living being has an electric field.

filter feeding—a method of feeding in which food is strained from the water and then swallowed

gill rakers—thousands of fine bristles in the whale shark's throat; gill rakers strain plankton and fish eggs from water.

harpoon—to hunt large fish with long spears that are thrown by hand or shot from a gun

migrate—to move from one place to another, often with the seasons

overfishing—greatly reducing the number of fish in an area by fishing too much

ovoviviparous—producing young that develop in eggs inside the body; ovoviviparous animals give birth to live young.

pectoral fins—a pair of fins that extend from each side of a fish's body

plankton—tiny plants and animals that drift with ocean currents

spawning—the releasing of eggs into the water

vulnerable—at risk of becoming endangered

TO LEARN MORE

At the Library

Burnham, Brad. *The Whale Shark*. New York, N.Y.: PowerKids Press, 2001.

Musgrave, Ruth. *National Geographic Kids Everything Sharks*. Washington, D.C.: National Geographic, 2011.

Randolph, Joanne. *The Whale Shark: Gentle Giant*. New York, N.Y.: The Rosen Pub. Group's PowerKids Press, 2007.

On the Web

Learning more about whale sharks is as easy as 1, 2, 3.

1. Go to www.factsurfer.com.

2. Enter "whale sharks" into the search box.

3. Click the "Surf" button and you will see a list of related Web sites.

With factsurfer.com, finding more information is just a click away.

INDEX